CLASSIC BOATS
Nigel Sharp

AMBERLEY

Photographs by the author

First published 2017

Amberley Publishing
The Hill, Stroud
Gloucestershire, GL5 4EP

www.amberley-books.com

Copyright © Nigel Sharp, 2017

The right of Nigel Sharp to be identified as the
Author of this work has been asserted in accordance
with the Copyrights, Designs and Patents Act 1988.

ISBN 978 1 4456 6670 9 (print)
ISBN 978 1 4456 6671 6 (ebook)

British Library Cataloguing in Publication Data.
A catalogue record for this book is available from
the British Library.

Typeset in 9.5pt on 11pt Celeste.
Origination by Amberley Publishing.
Printed in the UK.

Introduction

What is a classic boat? There is no authoritative definition, of course. The *Oxford Dictionary* defines the adjective 'classic' as 'first class; of lasting value and importance' and that could easily be applied to the word in the context of boats, although it is generally simply a matter of opinion.

In 2013, the magazine *Classic Boat* ran a two-part feature on the subject, having asked thirty experts (boatbuilders, boat designers, boat owners, museum curators, photographers, journalists, etc.) their opinions on what defines a classic boat, and the result was, perhaps inevitably, thirty (more or less) different answers.

There were various views regarding age (for instance, some said pre-Second World War; some said pre-1970s; some said any age) and materials (all said wood, some said only wood; some said steel is OK; some said GRP definitely isn't; some said anything is) but here are some specific quotes that ring true to me.

'... endearing and enduring...' (Dan Houston, the then-editor of the magazine).

'Like beauty, a classic boat is in the eye of the beholder, or perhaps in the mind's eye...' (Robin Gates, a previous editor of the magazine).

'... an attribute always hard to define but universally recognised.' (Olin Stephens, the legendary yacht designer).

'Instantly recognisable, a classic has elegance, style, beauty, craftsmanship, quality of finish, and timelessness. She sits on, and moves through, the water with grace.' (Jonathan Griffin, curator of National Maritime Museum Cornwall).

'In my view a classic yacht must have a magic and a personality ... Maybe these are boats we fell in love with as children and have always wanted to own, or those that simply cast their spell and touch us as we walk along the dock with or without any knowledge of yachts or the sea.' (Barney Sandeman, yacht broker specialising in classic boats).

'I consider a classic boat to be one that has achieved the goal of combining beauty with functionality and one which transcends the whims of fashion...' (Andrew Wolstenholme, naval architect).

Not every boat in this book will have all of these qualities, but in most people's eyes I think that they will all have most of these qualities. The majority are of timber construction – traditional plank-on-frame, modern epoxy-based methods and everything in between – but there are also boats built of steel, aluminium and GRP, and even two of ferro-cement. And age is no barrier as far as I am concerned: the oldest boat included is the 1860 *Mermaid,* which is in company with over thirty other centenarians, but there are almost as many which were built in the twenty-first century.

The classic boat revival of the past thirty years-or-so has been quite phenomenal. It has provided a great many people with entertainment, sport, employment, exercise and glorious spectacles that seemed destined never to be witnessed again. But most importantly it has saved countless old boats from watery graves and created many more new ones.

A note regarding the lengths of boats: there was a time when writers would always refer to waterline lengths because that is the factor that governs theoretical maximum speeds.

Nowadays overall length is universally quoted, not least because there is often a need to portray a boat in the best possible light from a 'selling' point of view. But therein lies potential confusion, particularly in the case of a gaff cutter, which may have a bowsprit and boom protruding beyond the extremities of the hull. When some people write length, or length overall, they might mean the length of the hull, while others might mean the length over spars. Throughout this book, unless otherwise stated, length means 'length over spars' in the cases of boats that have bowsprits and protruding booms.

A further note, regarding photographs: it isn't quite true to say that all the photographs in this book were taken by me, but all but one were and they were all taken with one of my cameras. When I met up with the owner of the cat-rigged *Lucie* on the banks of the Thames at Pangbourne in 2012, he told me that he wasn't particularly confident sailing his own boat but that he would be quite happy to operate my camera, so we reversed our intended roles.

In their working days – between the early nineteenth and the early twentieth centuries – Falmouth Quay Punts provided an essential service to visiting ships: transportation of supplies, messages, and crew to and from the town, as well as pilotage. *Matahari* was built by R. S. Burt of Flushing, near Falmouth, in 1930, along the lines of a Quay Punt but as a cruising yacht, for which many of the Quay Punt's characteristics – seaworthy, suitable for shorthanded sailing, relatively fast and with roomy hulls – were highly desirable. In the early 1990s her then-owners sailed her to the Baltic, Brazil, the West Indies and Maine before bringing her back to Cornwall where she has been based ever since.

Sumurun was designed and built by William Fife III in 1914 as a gaff yawl. Soon after the Second World War her first engine was fitted, and in the 1950s she was converted to a Bermudan ketch, initially with a small bowsprit. Her various racing successes include prizes in two Rolex Transatlantic Challenges: overall victory on corrected time in 1997, and first in the Classic Division in 2003. This photograph shows her sailing off Cannes in 2016.

Farouk was built by Cockwells Modern & Classic Boatbuilding, near Falmouth in 2014, and is based on the Andrew Wolstenholme-designed Duchy 27 but with a custom deck and cabin layout.

The photograph above shows an International 12 – a class designed by George Cockshott in 1913 and adopted for the Olympic Games in 1920 and 1928 – which was built in Germany in 1930.

Cuilaun was the first boat to be designed by George McGruer – the fourth generation of the Scottish boatbuilding dynasty – and was built at the family yard in 1970. She has crossed the Atlantic at least eight times, and she survived not one, but two, devastating fires when stored ashore in the USA. She is seen here taking part in the Pendennis Cup in 2014.

Cambria was designed and built in 1928 by William Fife III specifically to race with the so-called Big Class, which included King George V's cutter *Britannia*. She was dis-masted during an Atlantic crossing in the 1970s and she then had a prolonged refit in the Canaries; soon after that she was based in Australia for a number of years. Originally a Bermudan cutter, she became a ketch during this period, but she was converted back again in time to take part in the America's Cup Jubilee in Cowes in 2001. She is seen here taking part in Les Regates Royales in Cannes in 2016.

In 1907 at a conference in London, the International Yacht Racing Union was formed, and at the same time the International Rule was adopted. This led to the establishment of the so-called Metre classes, the names of which do not reflect the classes' overall lengths, but are the result of a fairly complex formula involving a number of different measurements. A century later, in July 2007 and immediately prior to a Centenary Regatta for various Metre classes, the 6-Metre World Championships were held in the Solent. Forty-eight boats competed – the largest gathering of 6-Metres ever seen in the Solent – of which twenty-five raced in the Classic Division, including the four boats pictured on these pages. *Nada* (K12) was designed and built by William Fife III in 1929, and *Caprice* (GBR48) – another Scottish boat – by James McGruer in 1946. At the 2007 World Championships they came thirteenth and third respectively.

Carrin II (CAN8) was originally called *Alice* when she was designed by Gosta Kyntzell and built by Wilenius in Finland in 1936, while *Titia* (GBR22) was designed by David Boyd and built by Woodnutts on the Isle of Wight in 1952 before taking part in the Olympics – the tenth and last time the class competed at the Games – later that year. At the 2007 World Championships they came tenth and fourth respectively.

Built as *Jessica* in 1984 by Astilleros de Mallorca to an Arthur Holgate design, this 212-foot (65 m) three-masted schooner was subsequently owned by Australian Alan Bond – perhaps most famous for lifting the America's Cup in 1983 – who called her *Schooner XXXX*. Her current owner changed her name to *Adix* when he bought her in 1989. She is seen here taking part in the 2014 Pendennis Cup in Falmouth, Cornwall.

Trasnagh was built by John Hilditch of Carrickfergus in 1913. She was one of six Island Class One Designs that were designed by Alfred Mylne, all named after islands in Strangford Lough. In their early days, the class would race at the Royal Northern YC on the Clyde and at the Royal Ulster YC on alternate weekends. Originally rigged as gaff yawls, the whole class was converted to Bermudan in the early 1920s, but *Trasnagh* was converted back again during a recent restoration. She is seen here sailing off Dartmouth in 2016.

Velacarina is a Truly Classic 85 that was designed by Hoek Naval Architects and built by Claasen Shipyards in Holland in 2004. She has an aluminium hull and carbon fibre spars. These photographs show her taking part in the Pendennis Cup in 2012 (above) and in 2014 when she was the overall winner.

The Sunbeam was designed by Alfred Westmacott in 1922. Two fleets soon became established, in the Solent and Falmouth where they first raced in 1923 and 1924 respectively. Forty-eight have now been built and all but one survive today. The fleet is split roughly equally between the two areas and, while the Solent Sunbeams – based at Itchenor in Chichester Harbour – allow spinnakers, the Falmouth boats have an unusual system called the kitty gear, which allows the jib tack to be poled out easily and efficiently when sailing off the wind. These photographs were taken at the 2016 Falmouth Sunbeam Championships in which fifteen boats competed: V20 *Verity* (above) was built by Woodnutts on the Isle of Wight – as were most of the Sunbeams – in 1926; and (below) eight boats – two of which still have their kitty gear deployed – approach the leeward mark.

William Fife III designed the Belfast Lough One Design, nine of which were built by John Hilditch of Carrickfergus in 1897. One of them was *Tern,* which first left Belfast Lough in 1901 and then had a succession of about a dozen owners who kept her at various ports in Scotland and Ireland before she sailed to Cornwall in the late 1950s. Five more owners in the Falmouth area followed and in 2008 she was taken to Mallorca, where she soon fell into a state of disrepair. In 2013 she was found by an enthusiastic yachtsman who had the means to have her extensively restored by a team of boatbuilders in Port Adriano. These photographs were taken in blustery conditions when she was taking part in Les Voiles de St Tropez in 2015. In 1897, Ratsey and Lapthorn's Gourock loft produced the sails for all the new boats and were under such pressure to do so before the first race that, when they found they didn't have a number 7 for *Tern's* mainsail, they used an upside-down 2 instead. When the same sailmaking company produced new sails as part of *Tern's* recent restoration, it was decided to replicate this.

These two photographs show two 12-Metres sailing off Cannes in 2016. *Seven Seas* (US9, above) was designed by Clinton Crane and built by Henry Nevins in New York in 1935. In the early 1990s she was extensively restored by Southampton Yacht Services and she has been based in the Mediterranean since then. *France I* (below) was France's very first America's Cup challenger. She was designed by Andre Mauric and built by Herman Egger for Baron Bich's 1970 challenge – Bich also built another new 12 and bought three existing ones, including *Sovereign*, Britain's unsuccessful 1964 challenger, to act as trial horses – but she was defeated in the challenger trials by the Australian *Gretel II*.

These two photographs were both taken during Panerai British Classic Week in the Solent in 2016. *Mikado* (above) was built as a Clyde Linear 30 – 30 foot on the waterline – in 1904 by William Fife III to his own designs. Originally gaff rig, she was converted to Bermudan in the 1920s. *Krabat* (below) was designed by Christian Jensen and built in secrecy at Anker and Jensen's yard in German-occupied Norway during the Second World War. Originally named *Tamara XI* she was launched in 1946, and spent most of her life based in Norway before recently moving to the UK.

Two sail-training boats are shown in these photographs. The 50-foot (15.2 m) ketch *Hardiesse* (above) was built in ferro-cement to a Percy Dalton design in 1972 and is based in Falmouth, Cornwall. Every year she takes young people on voyages around the West Country and across to Brittany, and she is seen here taking part in Falmouth Classics in 2015. *Donald Searle* (below) is an Ocean 75 ketch that was built in 1979 for the London (now Rona) Sailing Project, and is based on the Hamble River. She is named after the man who co-founded the MFI furniture business and whose legacy helped to pay for her after he died in a gliding accident at the age of fifty-two. Each year her programme typically includes sixteen week-long sail training voyages for teenagers, and various other voyages for people of all ages with special needs. It is estimated that around 18,000 people have sailed on her since she was built.

India is a Norfolk Broads Cruiser that was designed by Andrew Wolstenholme and built by Paul Bown in 2013. Her hull is strip-planked in western red cedar and she is a near sister ship of a cold-moulded boat built for the same owners in the late 1970s. She is seen here sailing on Barton Broad, Norfolk, a few weeks after her launch.

Nineteen 15-Metres were built in the seven years between the introduction of the International Rule and the outbreak of the First World War. Three were to the design of Alfred Mylne and four were by Charles E. Nicholson, but it is entirely appropriate that the four surviving boats were all designed and built by William Fife III, who originally produced a total of seven. All four have been extensively restored in recent years and now regularly race against each other in Mediterranean classic yacht regattas. These two photographs show *The Lady Anne* (D10) – currently in the same ownership as the three-masted schooner *Adix* – sailing in Falmouth Bay in 2008 (above) and in St Tropez in 2011 (below).

These photographs were both taken in St Tropez in 2015. The one above shows the 15-Metre *Mariska* (D1) racing in brisk conditions, while all four surviving 15-Metres – including *Tuiga* (D3), which is now owned by the Yacht Club de Monaco, and *Hispania* (D5), which was originally built for the King of Spain – are moored together stern-to (below).

Since the middle of the nineteenth century oysters have been harvested in the Fal estuary and, in order to preserve the stocks and protect the beds from over-fishing, a bye-law still, to this day, prevents oyster fishermen from using engines when dredging. During the last century and a half, well over 200 different vessels – Falmouth Working Boats, as they have come to be known – have dredged for oysters under sail in these waters in the winter months, and a great many of them have also taken part in local races in the summer. The Falmouth Working Boat *Alf Smythers* was designed by Percy Dalton and built in 1971. She has been used for oyster dredging ever since then, and for several years she also raced – almost the only active oyster dredging boat to do so in recent years. She is seen here racing in the Silver Oyster race in 2014 and dredging for oysters a couple of weeks later.

These photographs show two Falmouth Working Boats, which were both built in the Fal estuary in the nineteenth century and spent much of their lives dredging for oysters. They are now both owned by St Mawes-based syndicates, which use them for racing, and they are both seen here in the Carrick Roads between St Mawes and Falmouth. *Florence* (above) was built by William 'Foreman' Ferris in Pill Creek in 1895, and *Evelyn* (below) by Frank Hitchens in Restronguet Creek just three years later.

The 182-foot (55.5 m) schooner *Adela* was designed by Dykstra Naval Architects and built by Pendennis Shipyard in Falmouth, Cornwall, in 1995. Her original overall length was 166 feet (50.6 m) but Pendennis extended her in 2000 by cutting the hull in half and inserting a new midships section. Both these photographs show her racing in 2012: in the Pendennis Cup with part of Black Rock in the foreground (above), and in the Superyacht Cup in the Solent, with her massive 10,000 square foot spinnaker, affectionally known as 'the Big Red' (below). When she races she needs a crew of between thirty-five and forty people.

These photographs show two near-sister ships – albeit of different sizes – both built to Jack Laurent Giles designs and seen here taking part in Panerai British Classic Week in 2016. The 58-foot 6-inch (17.8m) yawl *Lutine of Helford* (above) was built in 1952 for Lloyds Yacht Club by Camper & Nicholsons at Gosport (who also produced her replacement, a GRP Nicholson 55, in 1970). The slightly smaller (51-foot/15.5-metre) *Le Rayon Vert* (below) was built in Holland in 2001.

Over a century ago, working boats of different types based in Beer in East Devon began putting commercial interests to one side for one day every August so that they could race each other in Beer Regatta. From these origins came the formation of Beer Luggers Club in 1985 and a subsequent expansion of the racing programme. Races are now held every Monday evening throughout the summer, and the photograph above shows one such evening in 2010 wherein a group of lugger sailors stand near their partially rigged boats and wait to see if there will be enough wind to allow them to sail. The photograph below shows *Scrumpy* – built in 1968 as a cabin cruiser – taking part in the race that did eventually take place that evening.

These photographs were taken during another Monday evening Beer Lugger race, in 2015. *Gannet III* (above) had been built by Fowey boatbuilder Peter Williams just a year earlier, and (below) she leads *Twilight* (18) and *Percy Mitchell* (14) away from the start.

The Bermudan ketch *Eilean* was designed and built by William Fife III in 1936. In 1982 the pop group Duran Duran chartered her so that they could film a video for their hit single 'Rio' on board her. In 2006, when she was lying in a dilapidated state in Antigua, she was purchased by watchmakers Panerai and extensively restored. Since then she has been Panerai's flagship, and she is seen here taking part in one of the many classic yacht regattas sponsored by the company, in Cannes in 2016.

The 36-foot 11-inch (11.2 m) *Sunmaid V* was designed by Sparkman & Stephens and built by Clare Lallow in Cowes in 1967; she is seen here taking part in Panerai British Classic Week in 2016.

The Spitfire 18 was designed by Ted Spears and built in 2013 by his company North Quay Marine at Conyer in Kent. Her hull is constructed of tongue-and-groove cedar strip planking, epoxy sheaved. The name of the boat comes from the shape of her mainsail, which has a very pronounced curved gaff and is thought to resemble a Spitfire wing. This photograph shows the prototype, *Ryan's Racer*, sailing on the Medway.

The 6-Metre *Sun Ray*, which was built by Jorgen Jensen in Copenhagen in 2005 to a 1936 Arvid Laurin design, taking part in the 2007 6-Metre World Championships, in which she came second in the Classic Division.

Throughout the nineteenth and the very early part of the twentieth centuries, Pilot Cutters played a vital part in the safety of shipping around our coasts. Ships have always needed a pilot's local knowledge to guide them in and out of our ports and the cutters' role was to ensure that the pilots were on board at the right time and in the right place. The requisite characteristics of a Pilot Cutter – easily handled by a small crew, fast to give them a better chance of reaching the ships first and so securing the business, and extremely seaworthy to be able to go to sea and stay there in whatever conditions prevailed – are all highly desirable in cruising boats today, and in recent years there has been a resurgence of interest in these boats. With a hull length of 48 feet (14.6 m), *Merlin of Falmouth* is a slightly extended replica of the Bristol Channel Pilot Cutter *Peggy*, which was built by Edwin 'Cracker' Rowles of Pill, near Bristol, in 1904. *Merlin* was traditionally built, with larch planking on oak frames, at Cockwells Modern & Classic Boatbuilding in 2010. These photographs show her on sea trials soon after she was built.

The Bristol Channel Pilot Cutter *Mascotte* was built in 1904 by her first owner and pilot Thomas Cox and boatbuilder William Stacey. With a hull length of 60 feet (18.3 m) she was about 10 feet longer than most other Pilot Cutters, and this was so that she could accommodate three pilots, Cox himself and his son and his nephew. She served as a Pilot Cutter for just eleven years, until powered pilot vessels put her out of business. She was used as a private yacht until the mid-1950s – apart from the war years when she was laid up on the Hamble River – and then as a houseboat for about twenty years. In the mid-1990s she was extensively restored at Tommi Nielsen's yard in Gloucester, and she is now the largest surviving Bristol Channel Pilot Cutter. These photographs show her taking part in St Mawes Sailing Club's Pilot Cutter Regatta in 2013. The N on her mainsail denotes Newport, her home port in her working days.

In 1952, Silvers at Rosneath on the Clyde launched a 72-foot (21.9 m) motor yacht called *Thelma VI*, built to the design of the company's proprietor John Bain. For a few years in the late 1960s she was based in the Mediterranean, and about twenty years later she did some charter work for the BBC and is thought to have appeared in the television programme *Howard's Way*. She spent a decade-or-so as the unofficial floating clubhouse of the British Classic Yacht Club before the current owner purchased her in 2014, had her extensively restored at Stirling & Son in Plymouth, and renamed her *Life Aquatic*. She is now, once again, based in the Mediterranean.

Mermaid – designed and built in 1860 by Alfred Payne in Southampton – is thought to be the oldest racing yacht still in commission. She now has her original gaff cutter sail plan, which includes a massive 20-foot (6.1 m) bowsprit, but she has at various times also been rigged as a Bermudan cutter and a Bermudan ketch. Her current owner – her twenty-sixth – has spent almost twenty years restoring her, almost singlehanded.

Moosk was built in 1906 by W. E. Thomas & Co. of Falmouth. Originally rigged as a gaff yawl, she was converted to a Bermudan yawl at some point before the Second World War, and then back again in the early 2000s. Since 2012 she has been owned by The Island Trust, the Plymouth-based sail training organisation. This photograph shows her leaving Falmouth on her way back to Plymouth in 2016.

The 19-Metre *Mariquita* (overall length 125 feet/38.1 metres) was designed and built – with 2-inch/50-millimetre thick mahogany planking on steel frames – by William Fife III in 1911. She and three other 19s then enjoyed three seasons of competitive racing all around the UK, and also in Kiel and Le Havre, before the First World War intervened. Having spent twenty-five years being used as a houseboat on the River Orwell, she was rescued in the 1990s and then extensively restored by Fairlie Restorations on the Hamble River. She is thought to be the only 19-Metre to have survived and she is certainly the only one in commission today. She is seen here taking part in the Pendennis Cup in 2012.

These photographs show surviving examples of two one-design classes designed by Nat Herreshoff for the New York Yacht Club: the New York 30 *Linnet* (above) and the New York 40 *Rowdy*. (Herreshoff also produced designs for NY50s and NY70s, and in all cases the numbers reflect the boats' waterline lengths.) Eighteen NY30s were built in 1905, twelve NY40s in 1915 and two more soon afterwards, all by the Herreshoff Manufacturing Co. *Linnet* is seen sailing off Cannes in 2016, and *Rowdy* – with a Bermudan rig designed in 1927 by Herreshoff himself to replace the original gaff rig – off St Tropez in 2015.

The company Spirit Yachts was founded in 1993 and since then has been building a variety of classic-looking yachts – but with many contemporary features – between 37 and 100 feet long (11.3 and 30.5 m) at their base in Ipswich. Hulls are constructed with strip-planking and exterior diagonal veneers, all sheaved in epoxy; their modern underbodies include fin and bulb keels; and sails made from the very latest modern materials are flown from their carbon fibre spars. These two photographs show two Spirits taking part in Panerai British Classic Week in 2016: the 2001 Spirit 37 *Strega* (above) and the 2003 Spirit 46 *Helen of Durgan* (below).

The 8-Metre *France* was designed by Francois Camatte and built by Chantiers Chiesa, Cannes, in 1937. She is seen here sailing off the town of her birth in 2016.

Waterfly is another of George Cockshott's International 12s. Built in 1920, she was, for many years, based at Trearddur Bay Sailing Club in Anglesey where the class was locally known as the Insects. Her current owner first sailed her in 1956 and, after acquiring her again in 2013, had her restored as a rowing boat.

Just ten J Class yachts were built in the 1930s, in compliance with the 1903 Universal Rule and mostly to compete in the America's Cup. Of these, three survive today, and five new ones have been built in the twenty-first century. The photograph above shows (left to right) *Velsheda* (built 1933), *Rainbow* (2012), *Lionheart* (2011) and *Ranger* (2003) approaching the starting line at the J Class Regatta in Falmouth Bay in 2012, the first time the Js had raced there for seventy-six years; and the photograph below shows *Ranger* (J5) and *Velsheda* (JK7) when the class returned to Falmouth in 2015.

Ranger (pictured here in Falmouth in 2015) is a replica of the 1937 America's Cup defender of the same name – the so-called Super J – which beat the much-fancied British challenger *Endeavour II* 4-0, and was scrapped a few years later. The replica was built in steel by Danish Yachts.

Velsheda (off Falmouth in 2012) was designed by Charles E. Nicholson and built at his family's Gosport yard for W. L. Stephenson, the chairman of Woolworths, and was the only one of the 1930s Js that was never intended to take part in the America's Cup. After spending many years in a mud berth, she was rescued in 1984 and spent a decade-or-so doing charter work, mainly in the Solent and without an engine. In the mid-1990s she was rebuilt by Southampton Yacht Services and has been racing competitively ever since.

Rainbow (off Falmouth in 2012) is a replica of the 1934 Starling Burgess-designed America's Cup defender of the same name, which beat *Endeavour* 4-2. She was built in aluminium by Holland Jachtbouw in 2012 to a design optimised by Dykstra Naval Architects.

In 1937, Starling Burgess and Olin Stephens produced eight designs between them as possible challengers for the America's Cup. Ranger was the only one to be built until 2011 when another of them – *Lionheart*, pictured crossing the finishing line off Falmouth in 2015 – was built in aluminium by Claasen Shipyards.

The first Fowey River boat was built in 1950 and was based on the *Yachting World* 15 ft Knockabout Boat. Five years later the class had its own start in Fowey Regatta Week and by 1965 thirty-six boats had been built. However, the class then started to go into decline, at least until the early 1990s when something of a revival began, and a total of sixty-seven boats have now been built. More than fifty are still based in Fowey – twenty-five of which took part in Fowey Regatta week in 2016 – while another half dozen-or-so are thought to have survived elsewhere. The photograph above was taken soon after the start of an evening race in 2016, and the one below shows FR64 *Cousin Jack III* in the same race.

In May and June 1940 about 900 vessels, of which around 700 were privately owned, evacuated 338,226 British and French troops from Dunkirk. The surviving boats became known as the Dunkirk Little Ships and the photographs on this page and the next two show some of them taking part in the seventy-fifth anniversary commemorative Return to Dunkirk in 2015. *Bluebird of Chelsea* (above) is leaving Ramsgate Harbour at the beginning of the Return. The 1922 Thames Sailing Barge *Pudge* (below) was one of thirty-or-more barges and lighters that went to Dunkirk. About a third of them failed to return, but this is largely because they were deliberately beached so that their cargoes of water, food and ammunition would be accessible to waiting troops.

This photograph shows the Thames barges *Greta* and *Pudge*, and the motor cruisers *Sundowner* and *Wairakei II*. *Sundowner* is particularly lucky to have survived: in 1940 – on her way back from Dunkirk with 122 troops on board – she was attacked by enemy aircraft; and in 1986 she was very nearly destroyed with a chainsaw before the intervention of the then-archivist of the Association of Dunkirk Little Ships.

By the time *White Marlin* was completed at her builders – Thorneycrofts of Hampton – in 1939, war had broken out, and she was immediately requisitioned by the Ministry of War Transport and renamed HMS *Fervant*. During the Dunkirk evacuation she was the Senior Naval Officer's launch and was one of the last naval vessels to leave the harbour.

In 1940, *Hilfranor* was abandoned at Dunkirk after sustaining damage in an attack by German dive bombers. It is said that she was later found by some desperate French soldiers, just as German troops were arriving, and they brought her back across the Channel. The crew of a minesweeper subsequently saw her sinking near the Goodwin Sands and towed her into Ramsgate.

The Little Ships – a total of forty-eight took part in the 2015 Return – gather in Watier Lock on the way in to Dunkirk Harbour.

Lucy Lavers is also a Dunkirk Little Ship. She is a Liverpool Class lifeboat, which was built by Groves & Gutteridge in Cowes in 1940 to be stationed at Aldeburgh in Suffolk, and the Dunkirk evacuation was her very first rescue mission. She ferried troops from Dunkirk's East Mole out to larger off-lying vessels, before being towed back across the Channel, laden with more troops. She remained in service at Aldeburgh until 1959, and during that time she was called out thirty times and saved seven lives. She then became a reserve boat serving at Wells-next-the-Sea twice, Sheringham, Flamborough and Rhyl, taking part in a further fifty-two rescues and saving another thirty-seven lives before being sold out of service in 1968. She spent the next thirty-odd years in Jersey, where she served as a pilot boat, a private fishing boat and a dive boat. In 2010 she was purchased by Rescue Wooden Boats, the Norfolk-based charity, and then extensively restored by brothers David and George Hewitt.

These photographs show her at Wells-next-the-Sea, where she now earns her living by taking members of the public on trips down the river.

In 2010 a Dutch yachtsman commissioned Hoek Naval Architects to design a boat that would recreate the beauty of the J class, but that would be as small as possible while still having the potential, with the help of contemporary features, to beat them in any conditions. The result is *Firefly*, which was built in aluminium by Claasen Shipyards and is seen here sailing in light winds off St Tropez soon after her 2011 launch.

The 33-foot (10.1 m) International One Design was designed by the Norwegian Bjarne Aas in 1936, and was based on his 6-Metre design *Saga*. There are now thought to be around 150 IODs actively sailing in half a dozen countries worldwide. This photograph shows the IOD *Kyla* sailing near Falmouth, Cornwall, in 2008.

Originally named *Moonbeam III*, and subsequently *Eblis, Moonbeam of Fife* was designed and built as a gaff yawl by William Fife III in 1903. Having been used as a refrigeration ship by German forces – who might alternatively have broken her up – in occupied France in the Second World War and having experienced a serious fire when later laid up in Southampton, her ongoing survival is particularly fortuitous. This photograph shows her sailing off Cannes in 2016.

The Falmouth Working Boat *Mildred* was built by R. D. Pill in Gorran Haven in 1913. For a period either side of the Second World War she had a Bermudan rig, and during the 1960s she was driven ashore and safely rescued on two occasions. It is thought that most of her owners have mainly used her for leisure purposes but she did dredge for oysters in the late 1960s and early '70s.

Esterel was designed as an 8-Metre by Leon Sibille and built by Chantiers De M Léon Sébille et Grossi, France, in 1912. These photographs show her sailing off St Tropez in 2015 (above) and off Cannes in 2016.

Charles E. Nicholson designed the 8-Metre *Folly*. She was built at his family's Gosport yard 'on spec' in 1909 when the International Rule had yet to establish itself, which is probably how she acquired her name. She is seen here sailing off St Tropez in 2015.

The two-masted lugger *Barnabas* was built in St Ives in 1881 for local fisherman Barnabas Thomas. Her registration number – 634 – was the number for 'Will Your Anchor Hold?' in the Methodist hymn book. She was owned and worked by three generations of the Thomas family for three-quarters of a century, and since 1994 she has been owned by the Cornish Maritime Trust, whose aim is to preserve her and sail her as much as possible. In 2015 she sailed around Britain, recreating the great fishing voyages she made in her early years.

These photographs are of two three-masted luggers, both replicas of historic vessels. *Grayhound* (above) is based on a revenue cutter of the same name which was built on the beach at Cawsand, Cornwall, in 1776. The newer boat was built in nearby Millbrook by a team led by Marcus Rowden and Freya Hart, who now run her as a charter boat. Her hull length is 63 feet 6 inches (19.3 m) – about 10 feet shorter than the original boat – but her length over spars is a massive 108 feet (32.9 m) and she can carry 3,500 square feet (325 sq. m) of sail. She is seen taking part in Falmouth Classics in 2015. The French bisquine *La Cancalaise* (below) was built in 1987 at Cancale as an exact replica of the 1905 *La Perle*, the last of the original bisquines which, in her day, trawled, fished and dredged for oysters in the Bay of Mont Saint-Michel. This photograph was taken at Looe Luggers Regatta in 2011.

Francis Chichester famously sailed *Gipsy Moth IV* around the world – stopping just once, in Sydney – in 1966/67. She then lay in a drydock in Greenwich for the best part of forty years before she was rescued and restored following a campaign led by *Yachting Monthly*. She has since been taken around the world again, but this time with numerous stopovers and crew changes.

Since 2011 she has been owned by the newly-formed Gipsy Moth Trust, whose aim is to protect and preserve her and to 'enable as many people of all ages as is practicable to see her and sail her' and she is seen here doing just that in Falmouth Harbour in 2013.

The 16-foot (4.9 m) St Mawes One Design was designed by Frankie Peters in 1923. Originally gunter-rigged, the class converted to Bermudan in 1953 and at the same time an extra 20 square feet was added to the sail area. To date forty-five have been built (twenty-four by Peters himself) and forty-one are known to have survived. The original boat – *Aileen* – is at the National Maritime Museum Cornwall. The photograph above was taken soon after the start of a race at St Mawes in 2015, and the one below is of *Vesper,* which was built by Peters in 1959.

The 138-foot (42.1 m) gaff schooner *Mariette* was designed by Nat Herreshoff and built in steel at the Herreshoff Manufacturing Co. in 1915. During the Second World War, she was requisitioned by the US Coastguard and sometime afterwards she was converted to a Bermudan staysail schooner. However, in the mid-1990s her original sail plan was restored and since then she has been raced competitively, mainly in the Mediterranean, although – as part of her centenary celebrations – she also took part in the Transatlantic Race, completing the Newport, Rhode Island, to Lizard Point course in twelve days, seven hours and twenty-one minutes. These photographs show her racing off St Tropez, where she is a regular visitor, in 2011 (above) and on her way to victory in the 2012 Pendennis Cup, in which she has now competed four times.

In 2015 Pendennis Shipyard in Falmouth completed the extensive restoration of the 165-foot (50.3 m) 1967 motor yacht *Malahne*. The project was managed by the company G. L. Watson, who were also contracted to design a new tender for her. The new 25-foot (7.6 m) boat was built by nearby Cockwells Modern & Classic Boatbuilding with a hull constructed of yellow cedar strip-planking with a Brazilian mahogany external veneer. She has a 286-hp inboard diesel engine, which gives her a top speed of 30 knots when loaded to capacity with eight passengers, but she can reach 38 knots with just a helmsman on board. She is seen here on trials off St Mawes, Cornwall, with her designer, Jack Gifford, at the wheel.

The Folkboat was conceived as a result of a design competition held by the Scandinavian Yacht Racing Union in 1942. *Orzel* (above) is a clinker Nordic Folkboat that was built in Szczecin, Poland, in 1963. Throughout her life she has been based on the south coast of England, in Flushing, Fowey, Lymington, Portsmouth Harbour and St Mawes. She has been owned by the author since 1998 and is seen here anchored in Frenchman's Creek off the Helford River. *Emily Grace* (below) is a carvel British Folkboat that was built by John Perry in Cosham, Hampshire, in 1961.

Dragon Fly was designed by Alfred Westmacott and built at Woodnutts on the Isle of Wight in the early 1920s. Since the mid-1990s she has been based in Falmouth, along with two sister ships.

Germaine is the oldest Camper & Nicholson yacht still afloat. She was designed by Ben Nicholson and built at the family's Gosport yard in 1882 and, after being found in a derelict state in a mud berth on the east coast in 1976, she was later restored at the International Boatbuilding Training College in Lowestoft. This photograph shows her taking part in Falmouth Classics in 2015.

Ripple is another two-masted lugger built in St Ives, by Henry Trevorrow in 1896. A serious engine fire put an end to her fishing career in 1933, and she was subsequently used as a houseboat on the River Fal for over fifty years. After an extensive restoration, she was re-launched in 2007 and has been actively sailing ever since, including here at the Looe Lugger Regatta in 2011.

More than 300 Brixham Trawlers were built in the latter part of the nineteenth century in the Devonshire town from which they take their name including, in 1895, *Pilgrim* (overall length 94 feet 6 inches/28.8 metres). She was kept in Scandinavian waters from 1912 until 1999, but since then she has been based back in Brixham. An extensive restoration – by Butler & Co. on the Dart and by about sixty volunteers – was completed in 2013, and she now earns her living from charter work. This picture shows her moored on the Dart in 2014.

Kensa was designed and built by Simon and Cat Holman in Portscatho, Cornwall, in 2012 specifically to allow them to fish commercially under sail. Her 18-foot 6-inch (5.6 m) hull is built of yellow cedar strip-planking, and she has a two-masted standing lug rig.

Bequia is a 90-foot 7-inch (27.6 m) yawl that was designed by Stephens Waring Yacht Design and built by Brooklin Boat Yard, Maine, USA, in 2009. Her hull is cold-moulded and is made up of six layers of Douglas fir and western red cedar veneers. These photographs show her racing in the Pendennis Cup in 2012.

Caramba was built in steel by J. Samuel White in 1963 to a Fred Parker design. She spent most of her life in the Mediterranean until her current owner bought her in 1999 and brought her back to the UK via the French canals. She is seen here in the Carrick Roads, near her base in Falmouth, Cornwall.

Outlaw was part of the three-boat British team which won the 1963 Admiral's Cup. She was designed by Illingworth & Primrose, and built by Souters of Cowes – her hull is cold-moulded and is made up of eight layers of mahogany – who launched her in April of that year. She was taken to the Caribbean and back in the late 1970s, and since the mid-1980s she has been based in the Mediterranean. This photograph shows her about to start a race at Les Regates Royales in Cannes in 2016.

The 60-foot (18.3 m) sloop *Pazienza* was built by Cantiere Navale V. Beltrami in Genoa in 1956 to a design by Jack Laurent Giles. Her first owner was proprietor of the Beltrami yard, but since about 1980 she has been based in the UK and has crossed to the Caribbean and back at least five times with four different owners. She is now kept on the River Dart and this photograph shows her taking part in the Dartmouth Classics Regatta in 2016.

The 34-foot 6-inch (10.5 m) West Solent One Design was designed by H. G. May (the proprietor of Berthon Boat Co. in Lymington) and H. Jacobs. Between 1923 and 1933, May's own company produced thirty-seven of them – five of which were exported to Argentina – and one other was built under licence in India. These photographs show the first of the class – W1 *Arrow*, previously named *Dart* and *Huahine* – sailing off Cannes in 2016 (above), and the 1931 W7 *Dilkusha* taking part in Falmouth Classics in 2015.

White Rose of Mevagissey is the first boat that Peter Moor – an experienced builder of fishing boats – built for himself, and the first sailing boat he built for anyone. He laid her keel in 2000 but, due to budgetary constraints and commercial work commitments, it wasn't until 2013 that she was completed. For her design, he drew his inspiration from *Wanderer II*, the gaff cutter designed by Jack Laurent Giles for Eric and Susan Hiscock in 1935. These photographs show *White Rose* sailing off Mevagissey in 2014.

The Fowey Troy class was designed by Archie Watty in 1928 specifically to sail in Fowey Harbour. Watty himself built the first fifteen boats and another thirteen have been produced elsewhere. All but two survive today. Watty built T13 in 1947. She was originally called *Little Gem*, then *Amber* and now *Solitaire*, all in accordance with the class's tradition of naming boats after gemstones. Fowey boatbuilder Peter Williams – who, incidentally, served his apprenticeship with a man who had helped to build T13 – extensively restored *Solitaire* in 2013, and she is seen here taking part in Fowey Royal Regatta Week soon afterwards.

The photograph above was taken soon after the beginning of a Pilot Cutter race from Fowey to St Mawes in 2013; and the one below shows the sterns of three Pilot Cutters – *Amelie Rose*, *Freja* and *Hesper*, all of which were built by Luke Powell at Gweek, Helford, between 2004 and 2012 – racing off St Mawes two days later.

It wasn't just the Pilot Cutters that went to sea to meet incoming ships for the purpose of putting a pilot aboard them. Pilot gigs – normally powered by six oars but occasionally by sail – were used for the same purpose and speed was of the essence for them as well. Since the mid-1980s there has been a significant revival in recreational gig rowing, not least thanks to the efforts of Ralph Bird, who not only helped to form the Cornish Pilot Gig Association, but also built twenty-nine new boats, two of which are shown here under sail in the Carrick Roads: Devoran Gig Club's *Fear Not* (built 1991) and Truro River Rowing Club's *Royal* (built 1998).

Kelpie was designed by Alfred Mylne and built by J. G. Fay & Co. of Southampton in 1904. She was one of eight so-called South Coast One Designs – although it seems they were not strict One Designs, and they shouldn't be confused with the Charles A. Nicholson design of the same name half a century later – otherwise known as SCOD 38s, as they had a waterline length of 38 feet. Sometime after the introduction of the International Rule in 1907, *Kelpie* was converted to rate as a 12-Metre and she then raced with other boats of that class for many years. She is seen here sailing off Cannes in 2016.

Halloween is said to have been William Fife III's first large Bermudan rig design, and she was built at his own yard in 1926, just in time to compete – and win line honours – in the second Fastnet race. In the 1950s – temporarily re-rigged as a yawl, renamed *Cotton Blossom IV* and in American ownership – she enjoyed great success in a number of ocean races. She is seen here taking part in Les Regates Royales in Cannes in 2016.

The gaff schooner *Morwenna* was designed by Linton Hope and built by Stowe & Sons in Shoreham in 1914. This photograph shows her sailing off Cannes in 2016.

Bojar is one of the last designs from the board of Norwegian Johan Anker. She was originally designed as a 90 Square Metre and was named *Ilmen V* when she was launched in 1937. She has spent most of her life in Norway but has been based in the Solent since 2012. She now rates as a 10-Metre, and she is seen here taking part in Panerai British Classic Week in 2016.

The 203-foot (61.9 m) aluminium schooner *Athos* was designed by Hoek Naval Architects and built by Holland Jachtbouw in 2010. She has a hydraulically operated centreboard and when it is lowered she draws 26 feet. These photographs were both taken in 2012 and show her racing in the Superyacht Cup in the Solent, with another big schooner, *Adela*, in the background (above) and in the Pendennis Cup (below).

In 1959 Morgan Giles designed and built seven 42-foot 6-inch (12.9 m) Bermudan sloops as sail training boats for the Royal Navy. Three of them – *Pegasus*, *Leopard* and *Gryphis* – are now owned by the Chichester-based company Classic Sail. In 2016, a group of Australian and New Zealand sailors flew half way around the world to charter all three boats and to race them in Panerai British Classic Week. These photographs show *Leopard* (above) and *Pegasus* taking part in that regatta.

Eda Frandsen was built in Denmark in 1939 to fish under sail in the Baltic. Soon after she was decommissioned in the late 1980s she was taken to West Scotland and converted into a gaff cutter suitable for chartering, although she was almost destroyed in a fire during the course of the work. She took part in four Tall Ships races in the late 1990s, and she now spends the summer seasons doing charter work in Cornwall and Scotland.

These photographs show two boats which were built by students at the Boat Building Academy in Lyme Regis in 2011. *Ellajen* (above) is a Selway Fisher Prospector canoe – the origins of which lie in Native American canoes that were adapted by gold prospectors in the seventeenth and eighteenth centuries – which is seen here at Dittisham, Devon. The photograph below is of *Lucie* – a 14-foot (4.3 m) version of a 21-foot 6-inch (6.5 m) catboat that was designed by the American Gil Smith in 1891 – sailing at Beale Park on the banks of the River Thames near Pangbourne (see note in introduction).

In 1946 Kenneth Skentelbery built a sailing dinghy called *Gannet*. This became the prototype for the Mayflower class, which soon became established in Salcombe and in Plymouth. Skentelbery's family company eventually built about a hundred timber boats, and several more in GRP. In 2010 Fowey boatbuilder Marcus Lewis built *Demelza* – the first new timber Mayflower for about twenty years – which is seen here sailing in St Just Creek in Cornwall in 2016.

The Redwing was designed by Uffa Fox in 1939, specifically for Looe Sailing Club in Cornwall. After the war its popularity spread and in 1947 it became known as the West of England Conference Redwing. Over 250 have now been built. This one, *Rosewing*, is seen here taking part in Falmouth Classics in 2015 with the 1926 Brixham Trawler *Vigilance* in the background.

Originally called *Negomi, Cerinthe* was designed by Kim Holman and built by Tucker Brown in Burnham-on-Crouch, Essex, in 1968. She is traditionally built with Honduras mahogany planking above the waterline and pitch pine below on steamed rock elm frames. Her first owner raced her keenly on the east coast for fourteen years, and since then she has been based on the south coast. Her current owners have kept her in Falmouth since 1992 and have cruised her extensively, including three voyages to the Caribbean.

The 53-foot (16.2 m) Sparkman & Stephens yawl *Skylark* – a near sister ship of the more famous *Stormy Weather* – was built in 1937. Having spent most of her life on the west coast of the USA she was extensively restored in Rhode Island in the early 2000s. These photographs show her racing off St Tropez in 2015 (above) and Cannes in 2016.

The 40-foot (12.2 m) sloop *Cereste* was designed by Robert Clark – thought to be along the lines of his famous Mystery design – and built by Sussex Yacht Works in Shoreham in 1938. She spent some time in the Mediterranean before returning to the UK in the late 1980s and then undergoing a thorough restoration about ten years later. She is now based on the River Orwell near Ipswich.

When the legendary designer William Fife III died in 1944, the yard at Fairlie – where the Fife family had been building boats since 1790 – was taken over by his protégé Archie MacMillan. The 1963 *Charm of Rhu* is an International 8-Metre Cruiser Racer which was designed by MacMillan and is thought to have been the last boat built at Fairlie before the yard closed.

Elena was built at Factoria Naval de Marin in Galicia, Spain, in 2009. She is a replica of the 1911 gaff schooner of the same name, which was designed by Nat Herreshoff and built by the Herreshoff Manufacturing Co. at Bristol, Rhode Island, USA. The original boat had a famously successful racing career, which included victory in the 1928 New York to Santander Transatlantic Race, and served with the British armed forces in the Second World War before being scrapped some time afterwards.

The new *Elena* regularly races in the Mediterranean classic yacht regattas, and in the three sailing photographs of her on these pages she is seen doing so in Cannes in 2016 with (above) her vast downwind sail area of over 19,000 square feet. The photograph below shows her moored up in St Tropez in 2015, and accentuates her massive boom, which, along with her bowsprit, gives her an overall length of 180 feet 5 inches (55.0 m), almost double her waterline length.

The first boats of the Falmouth 18 Foot Restricted Class were built in 1898 and, in total, just nine have been built to date. Six still survive, including *Magpie*, one of the original 1898 boats, and three in GRP. The only class rule was – and still is – that the hulls have to be 18-foot long, and this has inevitably resulted in vast sail plans and deep heavy ballast keels. These two photographs show four of the class racing off St Mawes in 2010: *Myrtle* (8) built in 1902, *Moey* (5), *Whisper* (32) and *Magpie* (2).

Moey (above) is a GRP 18-Footer built in 2010 from a mould taken from the 1930 *Marie*, but with extra freeboard which must have been welcome when this photograph was taken. *Whisper* (below) is another GRP boat, built in 1981 as a derivative of *Myrtle*. At that time *Myrtle* was in a terrible state and the intention was to destroy her as soon as the new glass hull was built, but happily a change of plan led to her ongoing survival.

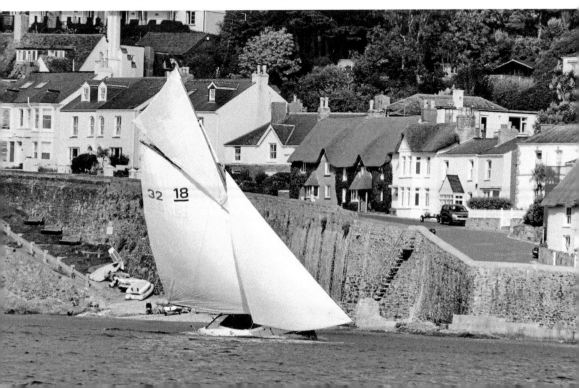

These two photographs show two contrasting examples of the 11-foot 6-inch (3.5 m) Iain Oughtred-designed Guillemot, both built at the Boat Building Academy in Lyme Regis in 2016. *Leaf* (above) is of clenched clinker construction – with Scottish larch planking and English chestnut ribs – and is gunter rigged; while *The Last Leg* (below) is cold-moulded and has a standing lug rig.

Drumfire (above) and *Heartbeat* are both Truly Classic 78s, designed by Hoek Naval Architects and built by Claesen Shipyards in 2006 and 2007 respectively. Although they both have aluminium hulls and similar layouts (on deck and down below), they are otherwise highly personalised. They are seen here competing in the Superyacht Cup in the Solent in 2012.

While the J Class are the biggest boats built to comply with the Universal Rule of measurement, there are many other classes denoted by other letters of the alphabet, right down to the S Class. The 61-foot 11-inch (18.9 m) double-ender *Serenade* is a Universal Rule N Class sloop that was designed by Nicholas Potter and built in 1938 by Wilmington Boatworks, California. Her first owner was the violinist Jascha Heifitz and many characteristics of the boat – the position of her winches, for instance – were conceived in order to safeguard his hands, which were reputed to be insured for a million dollars. *Serenade* spent much of her life on the west coast of the USA – where, it is thought, her guests may have included Humphrey Bogart, Lauren Bacall, John Wayne, Gary Cooper and Frank Sinatra – before moving to the Great Lakes and then Maine, and in 2015 she was brought over to the Mediterranean for the first time. These photographs show her racing in St Tropez later that year (above) and in Cannes in 2016.

The 90-foot (27.4 m) *Savannah* was designed by Pedrick Yacht Designs and built in carbon fibre in 1997 for an American yachtsman who was a particular admirer of the J Class and of the designs of William Fife III, and who wanted to recreate some of their visual characteristics in a modern yacht. She is seen here competing in the Superyacht Cup in the Solent in 2012 (above) and, two days later, with her crew in readiness for a fleet review by HM the Queen and HRH Prince Philip.

In 1854 seven Cornishmen – all related by blood or marriage – sailed the Mounts Bay lugger *Mystery* from Newlyn via Cape Town to Australia in search of gold. In 2008, *Spirit of Mystery* – a near replica of *Mystery* – was built at Millbrook in Cornwall for Pete Goss who then set off to recreate the 1854 voyage with his brother, brother-in-law and 14-year-old son. *Spirit of Mystery* arrived safely in Melbourne in March 2009, but only after putting in to Portland, Victoria, to disembark a crew member who had broken his leg in a 90-degree knockdown. This photograph shows *Spirit*, under new ownership, sailing off Cawsand, Cornwall, in 2015.

Designed by Sparkman & Stephens, and built by Lallows of Cowes in 1965, *Firebrand* was part of the winning British Admiral's Cup team that same year. In 1998 she was purchased by the yacht designer Ed Dubois who found her in Florida, and she is seen here taking part in the 2012 Pendennis Cup in which she won the Little Dennis class.

The 10-Metre *Marga* was designed by C. O. Liljegren and built at the Swedish Hästholm Boatyard in 1910. Two years later she represented Sweden in the 10-Metre class at the Stockholm Olympic Games: she finished 4th out of 4 in both races although another Swedish boat – the Alfred Mylne-designed *Kitty* – won the gold medal. She completed a five-year restoration in 2015 and this photograph shows her racing at Cannes the following year.

The 8-Metre Cruiser Racer *Freyja* – designed by Norwegian Erling Kristofersen in 1950 – taking part in Panerai British Classic Week in 2016.

These photographs show Falmouth Working Boats racing in Falmouth Week in 2013: (above, left to right) *Agnes*, *Grace*, *Winnie* and *Florence*; and (below, left to right) *Evelyn*, *Cousin Jinny*, *Victory* and *Rita*. Four of these eight boats were built in the nineteenth century.

These photographs show another pair of boats built at the Boat Building Academy in Lyme Regis. *Daydream* (above) is a plywood Golant Ketch that was designed by Roger Dongray – perhaps more famous for the Cornish Crabber and Cornish Shrimper – and is the first of her class; and *Lashanna* (below) is a Haven 12.5 that was originally designed by Nat Herreshoff in 1914, but then reconfigured with a centreboard, a shallower keel and Bermudan rig by Joel White in 1987.

Ocean Pearl was built as a motor fishing boat by Nobles of Fraserburgh in 1933. Her fishing career ended in 1967, and in the late 1990s she was rescued from a disused tarmac works near Staines in Middlesex. After a lengthy restoration, she first sailed with her new two-masted standing lug rig in 2007. She is seen here taking part in the Looe Luggers Regatta in 2011.

Jolie Brise was built as a pilot cutter in Le Havre in 1913. It wasn't long, however, before the advent of powered pilot boats led to a change of role: she served as a fishing boat for a while and then, from 1923, as a private sailing yacht. Two years later she famously won the first Fastnet Race, and she won it again in 1929 and 1930. She has been extensively used as a sail training boat by Dauntsey's School since 1977 when she was leased from her then-owners, the Exeter Maritime Museum, until 2003 when the school purchased her.

The 133-foot 10-inch (40.8 m) schooner *Altair* was designed and built by William Fife III, and launched in May 1931. Her original owner's brief to Fife was for 'a sound, safe cruiser; safe to go to the South Sea Islands with no difficulty', although he was never able to undertake such a voyage. In 1987 Southampton Yacht Services completed a restoration that is widely acknowledged as being ground-breaking, in that it paved the way for the restorations and rebuilds of numerous other classic yachts. This photograph shows her taking part in the 2008 Pendennis Cup.

Sparkman & Stephens became particularly well-known for their yawls in the 1930s, and in 1939 they designed *Enterprise*, which was built at Jacob's Boatyard, City Island, New York. After the war she was taken to the west coast of the USA and renamed *Adios*, but then her original name was restored when she later moved to the Mediterranean, where she is now based. This photograph shows her racing off Cannes in 2016.

Carron II is an 8-Metre, designed and built by William Fife III in 1935, and once owned and sailed by Prince Sadruddin Aga Khan. She is seen here sailing off Cannes in 2016.

The Ajax is a 23-foot (7.0 m) One Design class that was designed by Oliver Lee in 1966, and today there are well-established fleets at Harwich and St Mawes. This photograph was taken during a Falmouth Week race in 2013.

Three Bermudan yawls near the finish line at Les Regates Royales off Cannes in 2016.

Falmouth Working Boats at the start of a race off St Mawes in 2007.

Huff of Arklow is a Flying Thirty – 30 feet on the waterline and the only one ever built – that was designed by Uffa Fox and built by John Tyrrell & Sons of Arklow, Ireland, in 1951. Fox's drawings called for a much lower freeboard, but her builder and first owner, Douglas Heard, decided it should be raised to improve her seaworthiness and accommodation to allow offshore cruising. Her deck level aft, however, was kept low to allow Heard – who had sustained injuries as a Second World War fighter pilot – to board easily. During his thirteen years of ownership, Heard took her to Iceland and the Azores, and since 2004 she has been used as a sail training boat based in Plymouth Sound.

These photographs show yet more boats built at the Boat Building Academy in Lyme Regis. *Rosina May* (above) is a near-replica of a Thames skiff that was built by W. A. B. Hobbs at Henley-on-Thames in the very early part of the twentieth century. Workshop space at the Academy dictated that her maximum length was 21 feet (6.4 m), whereas the Hobbs boat was 3 feet (0.9 m) longer. The 22-foot (6.7 m) Nordland boat (below) – based on a traditional type of fishing boat that has been used for centuries in the northern part of Norway – was built in 2015.

In 1928, a gaff schooner called *Hopeful* – designed by Francis Sweisguth who was perhaps best known for the 1910 Star, the sixteen-times Olympic class keelboat – was launched at Harvey Gamage's Maine shipyard. She was subsequently renamed *Kelpie* and during the war she served as a submarine patrol vessel with the US Coast Guard's Coastal Picket Patrol off the coast of Maine. In 2012, by which time she had been re-rigged as a Bermudan staysail schooner, she was purchased by a man who already owned another classic schooner, *Mariette*. Despite being in poor condition, she was sailed from the west coast of the USA to Cornwall, where she was extensively restored on the Helford River. When the work was complete she was renamed *Kelpie of Falmouth* and, with her original gaff schooner sail plan replicated, she competed in the 2014 Pendennis Cup, which is where the photograph above was taken. The one below shows her off Cannes two years later.

Index